# Zoom in on
# TUNNELS

Kevin Reilly

**Enslow Publishing**
101 W. 23rd Street
Suite 240
New York, NY 10011
USA

enslow.com

# WORDS TO KNOW

**aqueduct**—A sloped tunnel that brings drinking water to towns and cities.

**aquifer**—An underground layer of rock, sand, or soil that contains water.

**engineer**—A person who helps to design and build tunnels or other structures.

**irrigate**—To give water in order to help growth.

**qanat**—A system of wells and tunnels for moving water, similar to an aqueduct.

**resources**—Important materials like coal, water, and oil that people use to make their lives easier.

**terrain**—An area of land.

**trench**—A long, narrow ditch.

**tunnel**—Any man-made underground passage longer than 75 feet (22 meters) and wider than 5.9 feet (1.7 meters).

# CONTENTS

Tunnels make it easy for people and resources to get from one place to another.

# What Are Tunnels?

You may not realize it, but tunnels are a very important part of your life! A tunnel is a man-made underground passage. Tunnels are built to help people and resources travel through difficult terrain. Some are beautiful and some are plain, but every tunnel is useful in some way. Let's look at tunnels a little closer and learn just how cool they are!

Even sewers can be tunnels!

## Parts of Tunnels

A tunnel is a long underground tube with an entrance and exit on either side. In the United States, any underground structure that is longer than 75 feet (23 meters) and wider than 5.9 feet (1.8 m) is called a tunnel.

If a tunnel is built for moving people, it may have a road, train tracks, or a canal running through it. If it is built for moving resources like water or minerals, it may only contain a small path for workers to walk on.

## The First Tunnels Ever Built

Tunnels have been around for thousands of years. Some of the earliest tunnels were aqueducts. They were built to get drinking water to people who lived in dry places or to irrigate crops. Others were simple sewer systems.

## Ancient Tunnels

Thousands of years ago, Persians began building qanats, underground tunnels used to get drinking water out of the ground. The deepest qanat, in Iran, still serves 40,000 people after 2,700 years! It is 1,180 feet (360 m) deep and 28 miles (45 kilometers) long.

# How Do We Use Tunnels?

Have you ever taken a long car ride through a hilly area?
Have you ever been on a train that went underwater?
If so, then you've already seen some of the ways that
tunnels make our lives better! Tunnels are used to help
people solve many different types of problems.

One way to get to New York City is to drive through the Lincoln Tunnel, which goes under the Hudson River.

## Transportation

Tunnels help us travel to lots of hard-to-reach places. They allow us to cross rivers and mountains quickly and easily. Can you imagine the world without tunnels? You would have to hike or fly across the Rocky Mountains. Manhattan would have a lot more bridges, and all the subways would be above ground!

## Gathering Resources

Some of the most important resources

## Getting to NYC

There are 23 tunnels in New York City alone. If they were replaced by bridges, there would be more than 80 bridges in the city!

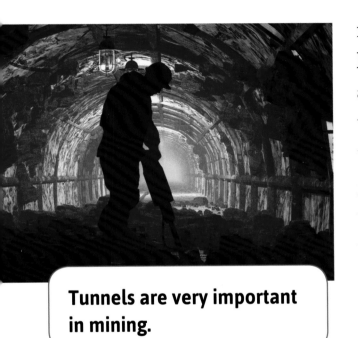

Tunnels are very important in mining.

for improving human life—like water and fuel—are also some of the hardest things for people to get. By using tunnels, miners can go very deep underground to find coal and other things that we use to power our cars and heat our houses. We also use tunnels to get drinking water from aquifers, or underground rivers, in places that don't have access to other types of water.

## Moving Resources

Getting to our resources is only half the battle. We also have to move them to places that people can use them! Tunnels can solve this problem in different ways. Some people live in dry places that are close to mountains. They often build aqueducts to take fresh water from the mountains and bring it downhill to the cities and towns. This method was used a lot in the past, but there are many examples of it still being used to this day!

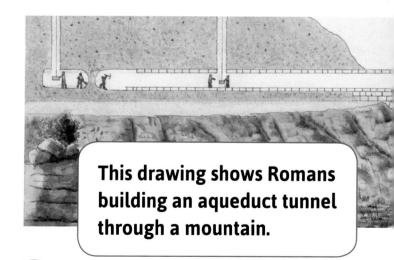

**This drawing shows Romans building an aqueduct tunnel through a mountain.**

# How Do We Build Tunnels?

By now you've seen how important tunnels are, and how we use them in many different ways. You're probably wondering, "How do they build these things?" First, an **engineer** comes up with a plan for the tunnel. It must be safe and work with the land around it. Then, the tunnel is built. There are three main methods used to build a tunnel: cut-and-cover, boring, and immersed tube. This chapter will take a look at each one.

Construction on the Gotthard Tunnel, the longest and deepest railway tunnel in the world

## The Cut-and-Cover Method

Some of the earliest tunnels were built using the cut-and-cover method. First, a deep trench is dug where the tunnel will go. Then, the trench is covered by a roof that can support the weight of whatever will be on top of it. These tunnels can cost a lot of money and usually disrupt traffic in the area for a long time. Today, they are not built very often.

## The Boring Method

The boring method for making tunnels is a lot more interesting than it sounds! Instead of digging an open trench, workers use giant boring machines to dig a hole through the ground. This allows life to continue normally above ground. It is also quicker and does not cost as much as the

## Big Moles

Tunnel boring machines are sometimes called "moles." The largest tunnel boring machine is the Martina, which weighs 4,500 tons and can bore a tunnel that is 51 feet (15.5 m) wide.

This huge tunnel boring machine is known as Big Becky.

cut-and-cover method. But boring machines are huge and expensive, which makes them hard to get and move around.

## The Immersed Tube Method

One popular way to build underwater tunnels is the immersed tube method. A huge tube is built in pieces somewhere on land. Then they are moved to

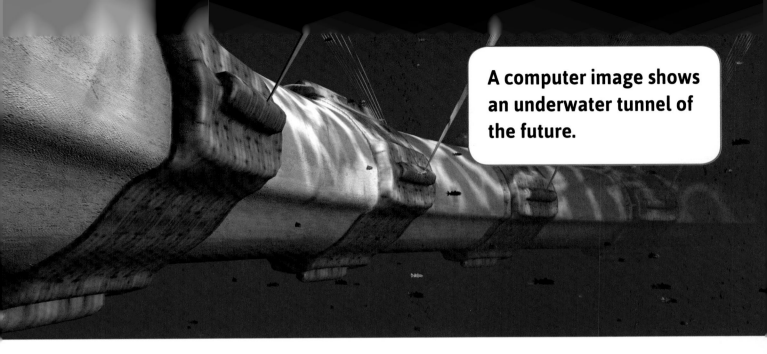

A computer image shows an underwater tunnel of the future.

the construction site and sunk. Once everything is underwater, construction workers link the pieces of tubing and pump the water out of the new tunnel. This is one of the fastest and cheapest ways to build tunnels.

# The World's Coolest Tunnels

All tunnels are cool, but there are some that deserve a closer look. These tunnels are the longest, deepest, most mind-boggling tunnels in the world! This chapter will show some examples of today's best tunnels. But if you do some research, you might find that another amazing tunnel is close to where you live!

Workers inside the Delaware Aqueduct fix a leak.

## The Delaware Aqueduct

At a whopping 85 miles long, the Delaware Aqueduct is the world's longest tunnel. It was built between 1939 and 1945 and brings 1.3 billion gallons of drinking water from the Catskill Mountains to New York City every day. The tunnel delivers more than half of the city's water supply. But there is a problem: It was recently discovered that the aqueduct leaks 36 million gallons of water a day! Now the government has started a

billion dollar project to repair the leaks.

## The Channel Tunnel

The Channel Tunnel—or Chunnel, for short—is definitely one of the coolest tunnels on the planet. It connects England with France by crossing the English Channel underwater. Only a few generations ago, this would have seemed impossible. The Chunnel is 31.4 miles (50.5 m) long, with a 23.5-mile (37.8-m) underwater section. It is the longest undersea section of a tunnel on Earth!

## The Busy Chunnel

The Channel Tunnel carries 21 million passengers and 20 million tons of freight between England and France every year!

The Eurostar bullet train allows people to travel underwater from Paris to London in only two hours. It goes through the Channel Tunnel, the longest undersea tunnel in the world.

# ACTIVITY
## PLAN YOUR OWN TUNNEL

Tunnels can be used to make life easier almost everywhere, even your own hometown! This fun activity will help you to learn how engineers think.

1. Take some time to look around your town for places that a tunnel might improve transportation. Is there a body of water nearby that makes travel more difficult? Are there hills or mountains that drivers avoid by taking long, winding roads? Could you design a straight path through your city that avoids traffic lights and buildings? If you answered "yes" to any of these questions, you've found the perfect place for a tunnel!

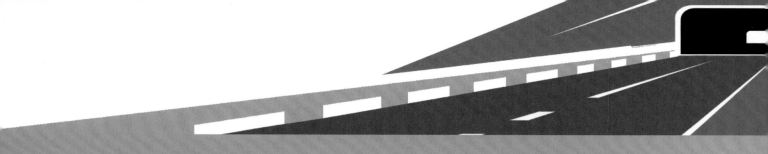

2. Now that you've found your location, try to decide which method of construction would be best for your project. You can look in chapter 3 for ideas, or do some research on a kid-friendly website with your parents' permission. Keep in mind the obstacles that your tunnel would avoid.

3. Finally, make a sketch of what your brand-new tunnel would look like once it's finished. Don't be afraid to get creative here, that's the best part!

Congratulations, you've taken the first steps toward becoming a real-life engineer: planning, researching, designing, and using your creativity to help make people's lives easier!

# LEARN MORE

## Books

Latham, Donna, and Jenn Vaughn. *Bridges and Tunnels: Investigate Feats of Engineering with 25 Projects*. White River Junction, VT: Nomad Press, 2012.

Mattern, Joanne. *Tunnels*. Vero Beach, FL: Rourke Educational Media, 2015.

Pettiford, Rebecca. *Tunnels*. Minneapolis, MN: Jump!, 2016

## Websites

**Easy Science for Kids**
*easyscienceforkids.com/all-about-tunnels*
   An accessible look at the basics of tunnels, with pictures and videos.

**How Stuff Works**
*science.howstuffworks.com/engineering/structural/tun. htm*
   A fun breakdown of the science behind tunnels.

# INDEX

Published in 2018 by Enslow Publishing, LLC.
101 W. 23rd Street, Suite 240, New York, NY 10011

Copyright © 2018 by Enslow Publishing, LLC.

Library of Congress Cataloging-in-Publication Data
Names: Reilly, Kevin, 1991- author.
Title: Zoom in on tunnels / Kevin Reilly.
Description: New York : Enslow Publishing, 2018. | Series: Zoom in on engineering | Includes bibliographical references and index. | Audience: Grade K-3.
Identifiers: LCCN 2017003023| ISBN 9780766087125 (library-bound) | ISBN 9780766088368 (pbk.) | ISBN 9780766088306 (6-pack)
Subjects: LCSH: Tunnels—Juvenile literature. | Tunnels—Design and construction—Juvenile literature.
Classification: LCC TA807 .R45 2018 | DDC 624.1/93—dc23
LC record available at https://lccn.loc.gov/2017003023

Printed in the United States of America

**To Our Readers:** We have done our best to make sure all website addresses in this book were active and appropriate when we went to press. However, the author and the publisher have no control over and assume no liability for the material available on those websites or on any websites they may link to. Any comments or suggestions can be sent by e-mail to customerservice@enslow.com.

**Photo Credits:** Cover, p. 1 (inset), p. 4 FocusLuca/Shutterstock.com; cover, p. 1 (background) aaabbbccc/Shutterstock.com; pp. 2, 3, 5, 8, 13, 18, 22, 23, back cover Vector Tradition SM/Shutterstock.com; p. 4 MartinMojzis/Shutterstock.com; p. 6 Jaromir Chalabala/Shutterstock.com; p. 7 Richard I'Anson/Lonely Planet Images/Getty Images; p. 9 Rana Faure/Corbis/VCG/Getty Images; p. 11 iurii/Shutterstock.com; p. 12 DEA PICTURE LIBRARY/De Agostini/Getty Images; pp. 14, 16 Bloomberg/Getty Images; p. 19 © AP Images; p. 21 EQRoy/Shutterstock.com; p. 23 Toltemara/Shutterstock.com; graphic element (blue tunnel icon) Rashad Ashurov/Shutterstock.com.